Wheels

Susan Canizares
Daniel Moreton

Scholastic Inc.
New York • Toronto • London • Auckland • Sydney

Acknowledgments

Literacy Specialist: Linda Cornwell

National Science Consultant : David Larwa

Design: Bryce Schimanski

Photo Research: Amla Sanghvi

Endnotes: Mary Hart

Endnote Illustrations: Craig Spearing

Photographs: Cover: Tony Freeman/Photo Edit; pg. 1: Jeff Greenberg/Photo Edit; pg. 2: Esbin Andersn/Image Works; pg. 3: Bob Daemmrich/Stock Boston; pg. 4: Roy Morsch/Stock Market; pg. 5: B. Christensen/Stock Boston; pg. 6: Blaine Harrington/Stock Market; pg. 7: Robert Brenner/Photo Edit; pg. 8: Bruce Berman/Stock Market; pg. 9: Joe Sohm/Image Works; pg. 10: Joseph Nettis/Stock Boston; pg. 11: Michael Newman/Photo Edit; pg. 12: Don Smetzer/Tony Stone Images.

Library of Congress Cataloging-in-Publication Data
Canizares, Susan 1960-
Wheels/Susan Canizares, Daniel Moreton.
p.cm. --(Science emergent readers)
Summary: Simple text and photographs present
wheels in motion, steering, turning, digging, and rolling.
ISBN 0-439-08123-8 (pbk.: alk. paper)
1. Wheels--Juvenile literature. [1. Wheels.] I. Moreton, Daniel. II. Title. III. Series.
TJ181.5.C36 1999
621.8'11--dc21   98-53309
CIP AC

2   3   4   5   6   7   8   9   10   08   03   02   01   00· 99

What do wheels do?

Wheels turn.

Steer, steer, steer.

Wheels turn.

Dig, dig, dig.

Wheels turn.

Ride, ride, ride.

Wheels turn.

Roll, roll, roll.

Wheels turn.

Spin, spin, spin.

Wheels turn round and round!

Wheels

Wheels are one of human beings' most useful inventions. One of the reasons is that a wheel turning on an axle is a very good tool for moving big loads. It is easier to move a heavy load with wheels than it is to carry the load or drag it on the ground. People first invented the wheel about 5,000 years ago. Before people had wheels, they moved heavy loads on sleds pulled by men or oxen.

What do wheels do? Wheels on airplanes roll down runways. Wheels on cars speed down the highway. Wheels on trains travel fast and far. All wheels go round and round.

Steer Steering wheels help drivers guide the car they are driving—turning the steering wheel turns the vehicle in the direction the driver wants to go. When you go spinning down the street on a bicycle, you use the bicycle's handlebars to steer and guide the bike. When your feet push the pedals around in a circle, the bike goes forward. Bicycle wheels have spokes to keep the wheels in shape. If the bike hits a stone or a pothole in the road, the spokes absorb the shock of the impact and prevent the wheel from buckling. Bicycles provide people with inexpensive, nonpolluting transportation. Bicycles are great for exercise and also lots of fun!

Dig More people work at farming than at any other job in the world. One of the most important machines on a farm is the tractor, which is used to move other field equipment. A tractor has two large rear tires that have treads. The treads grip the ground when the tractor pushes or pulls other machines. A cultivator is a machine that makes it easier for farmers to do their work. It has lots of little wheels with very sharp teeth that break up and turn the hard soil. The wheels also pull up weeds that sprout among the growing crops.

Ride A Ferris wheel turns in a circle. It carries you high up in the air, and then back down to the ground. You can ride round and round on a Ferris wheel at a fair, carnival, or amusement park. The world's largest Ferris wheel is the Cosmoclock 21 in Yokohama, Japan. It is 344.5 feet high—about as tall as the 34th floor of a building! It has 60 passenger cabs that can carry hundreds of people at one time.

Roll The wheels on a train are made of steel. Train wheels are grooved and are made specially to move fast on metal tracks. They can go much faster than a car. The French high-speed train is one of the world's quickest passenger trains. Trains are particularly useful for carrying heavy freight and for taking people to and from their jobs in city centers. Some passenger trains run underground, and some run on elevated platforms. The first trains were powered by a steam engine, but today almost all use electricity. If the tracks of all the world's main rail routes were laid end to end, they would circle the earth more than 116 times.

Spin Humans started using a wheel to make pottery thousands of years ago. Many archaeologists believe that the horizontal potter's wheel, used for spinning earthenware, was the first kind of wheel. The potter puts a ball of wet clay onto the center of the wheel. As the wheel spins, the potter shapes the clay by pressing it with his or her fingers. Pots, bowls, vases, and mugs are just a few of the things made on a potter's wheel.

Wheels turn round and round Wheels on skates make them glide smoothly. Wheels on chairs are a great invention for people who have difficulty walking on their own. Whether the wheel is used for steering, digging, riding, rolling, or spinning, all wheels turn around and around. Life would be a lot more difficult without the wheel!